theHiredProject.com presents:

Get the Interview! Get the Job!

The Job Hunter's Handbook

Get the Interview! Get the Job!

The Job Hunter's Handbook

No matter your situation, this handbook helps those with little employment history, not a lot of work experience, a criminal record, and the standard job seeker. This handbook has updated information that focuses on the current job market and economy.

ACKNOWLEDGMENTS

I'd like to say thank you to

My Lord and Savior, Jesus Christ,
who gives me life, love, health, and my strength

My mother,
who gives me guidance

My family and friends,
who help me through my days

Table of Contents

Introduction

Hello,

I'm Vivian, and I want to introduce you to my job search handbook. There are many handbooks out there, but this one compiles the latest information to help you achieve the career you want in this current job market.

Those with criminal records, changing career fields, recent college graduates, and the general job seeker will hopefully benefit from the tips and material in this handbook. I would like to think of this handbook as what you need to get a job or even a career (there is a difference). This is only the needed information, no fluff. I don't want to waste your time….I just want to provide the tools you need to go out and get the job you want. Thanks for making this small investment to get the salary you deserve.

I've tried several different methods to

get a job, submitting countless applications, networking, job fairs, and everything else you could think of. I've experienced many different types of interviews and have been successful at getting job offers. It's hard to get a job, because you are not the only one looking to get hired. Many others are seeking also. You may be in a rural area with limited jobs or a large city with a large population. Supply and demand is the job market.

As mentioned above, a job and career are different. A job is the short-term goal to gain skills and experience. A career is the long-term goal to build a future for yourself and family. In other words, a job is a task, and a career is your profession. To make things simple, I will use the terms interchangeably; however, the information works for the goal of getting a job or career.

In today's job market, you need

special skills to get an interview. I think of job searching like fishing. You gather all the equipment you need and find the best place to fish. You throw your bait (resume) out there into a pond of what you think are hungry fish (employers), but you start to realize there are others fishing in the same pond, and they may have better equipment than you, or they may have better techniques than you, or they may do things you are not willing to do to get these fish to bite, like take less pay.

You also have to remember you have to be there at the right time, because some of the best and biggest fish are caught with the right timing. For example, networking and being hired for a position that hasn't been listed yet is about timing. You don't have the same amount of competition when it comes to networking versus just throwing your resume out to a group of employers online and hoping they select you from a pool of thousands.

I have looked at some job listings where they post the number of those who have applied to some positions, and it's sometimes in the thousands. Those are hard odds, especially if you have those minor things that could be hindering you or if you don't do the small things to try to get your resume reviewed by the employer. Job searching, or what I like to refer to as job fishing, takes skills, and I wanted to put as many tips here as possible to increase your chances of getting an interview, so employers can truly see your worth.

How I increased my yearly salary by $20,000 just by getting a title change!

Several years ago, I decided to get out of the military after serving more than 6 years, but the question was, what do I do next? Going into the military only a month after completing high school gave me a new look on life. I grew up in a small country town in rural Georgia and knew nothing beyond Jacksonville, Florida and Atlanta, Georgia. The military trained and molded me into a whole new person. I gained skills and experienced things others my age couldn't dream of in those 6 years.

Once I left the military, I was still the person looking for my next mission of saving a life and proudly serving my country. During deployments and moving to different locations around the world, I was able to obtain my bachelor's in organizational management and my master's in business administration. This may sound great and a sure ticket to being hired for a dream job with a top-rated corporation, right? Wrong, after serving my country, I was unemployed for 7 months. I was able to obtain a job at a university as an Advisor Associate while living in Maryland, which was a massive pay reduction from my military days.

I quickly looked for ways to earn a comparable salary to repay the student loans that my military tuition assistance didn't cover and to pay the bills I acquired over the years. This was a major time of adjustment both with my career path and lifestyle. Continuing to be in my military mindset of picking up and moving, I decided to return to that small town in Georgia. I felt the decreased cost of living would work in my favor, but once I returned to the very room in my mother's house I left so happily over 7 years prior, I found that I was wrong.

I applied to over 300 jobs within a 50-mile radius, and four months later, I found myself in a very impressive position as an employment coordinator at a university, without the great payday. I couldn't believe where I was in my career. I was traveling a great distance for very little pay. So, I quickly searched for what's next. The pick up and move plan was still in effect, but this time, I wanted a job before I moved.

After speaking with a friend in California, I decided to visit. After my second visit, I decided I liked the west coast, and my job search started once again. I was able to land a job and decided to leave Georgia behind, once again, for the growth of my career. At this point, I was helping individuals with mental illnesses and criminal records obtain employment. I actually enjoyed what I was doing, but I was not making what I did while in the military, and I was thousands of miles away from my family and friends.

I explored California and truly enjoyed my time there, but I wasn't satisfied with my situation. California's cost of living was much like Maryland's, and I was looking for my next move. Yet again, I was job searching. I gained a lot of experience from my personal job search and working with those individuals. I knew I wanted to continue to help others obtain the employment they wanted and desired.

Looking for the right fit career is a challenge, and sometimes, you have to change your environment to gain the skills you need in order to gain your fit. After leaving California with all that I owned, I felt Maryland, which I considered my second home, was my best option to getting the career I wanted. My journey taught me some valuable lessons, like you must be in a location more than a year or two to advance with a company.

Networking starts to pay off as your relationships grow. On the other side of my travels, I've gain more valuable warm contacts. Once reaching Maryland, I decided it was time for me to grab what was meant for me and what I felt was success. I got a part-time job working in the field where I worked while in the military.

It's sometimes easier to use the skills you already have, instead of trying to break into something new. I had my MBA, but I lacked the years of leadership experience that most organizations were seeking to accompany it. So, starting part-time with my skillset was the key. I obtained a full-time job doing what I loved doing in California, which was assisting developmental disabled individuals obtain and retain employment. Neither of these positions were what I wanted to do in line with my MBA, and I still wasn't making my desired salary, but it put me in a place to gain more soft skills.

I started to implement what I was teaching others. I came up with my career goals from where I was currently working. I then formulated a plan of action and took action. I listed all my warm contacts in the Maryland and DC area and started to network everywhere I went. I surrounded myself with successful business-minded individuals and worked to build relationships.

After being back in Maryland for one year, I was able to obtain a position with a $20,000 yearly salary increase. I could finally say I made more than I did when I was on active duty. And it continued to improve. In this handbook, I give you all the tools you need to achieve your career goals. I have personally done what I list in this handbook that has helped me to reach my career goals. It took me many years to learn what I give you today. If you simply set your goals, make a plan of action, and utilize this handbook, you can start on your career path to success today.

Who is this book for?

I'm sure I'm not the first to tell you that obtaining a job is a job of its own. I hope this book will help anyone find a job or career they desire. Are you a new graduate and looking to start gaining experience in your field? Are you under-employed and looking to earn more to support your family? Are you unemployed and seeking a job in the current job market? Whatever your situation may be, it would be to your advantage to study and put this handbook into action to Get the Interview/Get the Job. Let's get to it!

Part One: GET THE INTERVIEW

Getting started: Get the Interview! Get the Job! So, you're probably wondering where to start. First, you have to determine what your personal needs are and your goals for your new job. Think about what you will be willing to do, your pay requirements, the distance you're willing to travel, and your available work schedule.

Looking on various job sites will give you some ideas of what jobs are in high demand and the salaries being offered. Evaluate your skills, experience, and education to see what job opportunities are possible that you didn't consider.

Identifying your skills. Identifying your skills is your ticket to getting the job you want. You must be able to articulate your abilities and expertise in a way that's desirable to the employer. Many people have a hard time informing others of their skills and abilities, as this may seem like bragging. You must master the art of effectively selling yourself, meaning letting the employer know what you have to offer the organization.

Organizations want the best employees, and their goal is to add an asset not a liability. In fact, it is important that you convey to your potential employer what your talents are. You should be able to sell your abilities and accomplishments to your potential employer. That is how you will get the job you want. It is important that you don't appear arrogant or condescending, but you should also avoid selling yourself short.

If the interviewer asks you about your strengths or what separates you from the other applicants, you should be readily able to give a good answer. Before going to the interview, your résumé should highlight your skills, accomplishments, and talents. Being prepared before the interview will allow you to feel in control of the uncomfortable situation and answer the questions confidently.

Type of skills. There are two main types of skills, hard skills and soft skills. Hard skills are tangible in the sense that these are things you do, for example: knowing how to operate different kinds of machinery, knowledge of a specialized computer program, ability to type fast, skills on using many types of tools, credentials regarding special crafts, etc. Soft skills are skills that are rather abstract in nature, like personal qualities. This may include the following: being a good team player, having the ability to work independently, being enthusiastic or organized and decisive.

❖ *TASK: Make a list of your previous jobs and list the skills and experience acquired*

Make a list of all the companies you have worked for and the things you learned from these jobs. There will be a lot of things to list, and you should be careful not to forget even the smallest things or activities that you were a part of or organized. List numbers, "I supervised 50 staff members."

It is also a good idea to list the volunteer activities you participated in and the experience gained. If this will be your first job, write all your volunteer activities, personal clubs, accomplishments, extracurricular, and anything that shows you have job related experience. Many employers are open to unpaid experience, plus it shows you have other valuable characteristics, such as helping others.

Examples:

Companies:	Job Position:	Experience Acquired:
Jo's Drive-In	Cashier	• Completed over 200 daily money transactions • Maintained excellent Customer Service to over 500 customers daily
Pete's Department Store	Manager	• Effective leader of 5 employees • Attentive to details, which resulted in over 12 loss prevention cases
Friendly Cleaning Service	Housekeeper	• Understand cleaning techniques, which allowed for training all new employees on MSDS standards • Time management skills allow for completion of all daily tasks in a timely manner

Master Résumé. Identifying your skills is the start of developing your Master Résumé. Once you have an idea of your prospective jobs and your list of experience, skills, and hobbies, it's time to start on the résumé. You will not be doing the traditional résumé at this point; you will be doing what I call a Master Résumé. The Master Résumé is one document of all those hard and soft skills from your list put into "résumé talk."

The Master Résumé will also consist of your mailing address history, previous places of employment, salary history, education, training, special skills, volunteer work, accomplishments, hobbies, interests, organizations, and reference information.

Once you have compiled this document, it will be your master for all your résumé writing and applications. One key mistake of job seekers is they use one résumé for all the jobs they apply for. With the use of the Master Résumé, you will be able to cut and paste your résumé to fit each job you apply for. Your Master Résumé, like all résumés, is never finalized.

This document will continue to change as you think of new skills, so don't put a lot of your valuable job seeking time into it. This document is going to save you time when applying for jobs, but you can continue to update it as needed.

Include a list of your hobbies. Although it might sound trivial at first, it is also helpful to list all your hobbies. There are a lot of skills that your prospective employer may get from your hobby list, which can also give an idea of your personality. For example, if you were part of the school's debating team, the employer may relate that to you having good analytical skills.

If you were a champion chess player,

the employer will have the impression that you are good at making critical decisions. Think about your daily routine and the things you do and often take for granted. Are you an organized person, who always keep your things in proper order? Are you an extrovert that can easily make friends in a matter of minutes? These may seem like ordinary things to you, but your future employer might think otherwise. This list will help you prepare for the interview. I will discuss this more later.

TIP: *Once you have an idea of what type of job you are searching for, you should look up the education, skills, and job description for several different job postings. Look for common terms used in the various job descriptions and use the same verbiage as the job descriptions in your résumés.*

❖ *TASK*: *Complete the Master Résumé in electronic format.*

Strengths and Weaknesses

When applying for a job, it's ideal to identify your strengths and weaknesses and get prepared to address them. Be careful not to get too confident, since this is one common mistake that plagues job applicants. Appearing too confident or as somewhat of a know-it-all will only get you labeled by your interviewer as unfit for the job.

❖ *TASK: Decide what career you want*

You should be realistic about your skills and the level of expertise you have with it. For example, if you indicate you are a very organized person, then you should be able to show this to the interviewer by being able to organize your thoughts and effectively use the time given for your interview.

It is important to know your skills when you are job searching. Putting that extra time into your Master Résumé would be the best way to analyze your level of skill and the experiences you will bring to each job you apply for. Keep in mind the Master Résumé is never final; once you think of a new skill you have to offer, add it to the list. Doing the bulk of the work up front will help with a smoother interview and articulating your answers to the interviewer.

The Master Résumé is a great tool to help you organize your thoughts for each interview and allow you to focus on the skills required for each job. This will make selling yourself to the interviewer easier.

THE JOB SEARCH

Hot Tips on How to Fish for Jobs

Prior to looking for the specific job that would be the best fit for you, learn how to market your talents effectively. This will help you gauge the possibility of landing the job you want.

1. Skills and interests should be evaluated personally. Use the list you already prepared.

2. Know your limitations. There are jobs that are too demanding that might not work for you or jobs that you may be overqualified for.

3. Plan to apply as soon as there is an inner instinct that tells you that you are willing and qualified.

The first thing that needs to be done when looking for a job is to prepare an impressive résumé, as we discussed previously. The résumé will depend on the type of job being applied for. There are times when certain employers require more than just a résumé. Be prepared to put more effort when applying, such as providing a cover letter or letter of intent. Every professional job you apply for expects to receive a well-written résumé.

After preparing the documents needed for the application, the next thing is finding vacancy announcements.

❖ **TASK:** **Make a list of companies in your target area and go to their website and search their job vacancies.**

Here's a job-fishing checklist to help you along your way:

- O Identify experience list
- O Identify prospective employers
- O Prepare documents (Master résumé, résumés, cover letter)
- O Make a schedule (Apply, apply, and apply some more)
- O Contact companies and/or employers (Unlisted opportunities – networking)
- O Get ready for an interview
- O Evaluate how the interview went and

any needed improvements

- ○ Follow up with interviewer
- ○ Start the new job!

Where to look

After drafting your Master Résumé, you can change your focus to deciding what field or career you want to apply for. Review the accomplishments in your list and partner it with the employment you are seeking.

Always take time to consider if your skills are relevant to the job that you are aspiring for and only list those accomplishments. I use work accomplishments, because you should state how you have successfully preformed those skills in the past. The Master Résumé will allow you to compare your accomplishments to the job announcement skills and compile a résumé quickly for each job.

Places to search:

1. Referrals/Networking
2. Online
3. Newspapers
4. Direct Employer Contact/Yellow pages
5. Temporary Agencies (Temp agency)
6. Job Fairs
7. Unemployment/One-Stop Centers
8. Library

Referrals/Networking. When you are searching for a job, aside from checking the ads in newspapers, internet, and bulletin boards, it is also helpful to ask for information from the people on a warm contact list. Having a referral from one of the company's employees can go a long way toward landing an interview.

A typical company may receive job applications in the hundreds and usually 35% to 60% of all job vacancies are filled by referrals. The odds of getting hired when you have a referral are very high if you have another 200 to 500 applicants going for the same position. If you do not know anyone from the company that may give you a referral, it is a good idea to network in different organizations, such as trade groups, social networks, colleges, and professional associations.

Remember, having a referral greatly increases your chances of getting the position. Building a network now will help with future endeavors. Meet people everywhere you go and stay in touch, because that person maybe a potential referral.

Tell everyone about your job search; networking is the key. Relatives and previous office or company co-workers will be able to give hints on job vacancies in their current companies. If anything is open or opens in the future, they may remember you're looking. These people might not have any vacant position in their company, but they certainly know someone who knows or needs a new employee. Many companies avoid using major job websites and mainly list their current job openings on their company webpage.

Warm Contacts

Usually, when you are looking for a job, you would ask for help from family and friends. You would contact these people to ask for information on current job openings, business opportunities, and tips.

Your family, relatives, and friends belong to your warm contact list. The warm contact list is the list of people with whom you have or had some personal association. A former classmate, officemate, or neighbor may belong to your warm contact list.

Who may be included in your warm contact list? Here are a number of selections.

* Relatives and Friends

These people are always willing to help you in your job search or business venture. They will be able to provide information if they have some or refer you to trustworthy people who will be able to help you. They may introduce you to some of their contacts and provide honest information to you regarding the person you're going to associate with.

* Members of the church, political party, social club, fraternity or sorority.

You probably did not expect it, but people who share the same faith, beliefs, or hobbies may also help you find a job. You may have a different career from theirs, but they might know somebody who is in the same field or be able to help you in your career.

* People who sell you things

You may think your relationship with these people is purely based on trading goods and services then paying for them. However, people who sell you things are also sources of information when networking.

Since these people sell their goods to different types of people, they may have associated with somebody who belongs to the same field as you do or have heard information about your target job from their other clients.

These people will also be happy to help you, since they know that maintaining a pleasant relationship with you means a stable business. Also, if you have a good job, it may mean you will have increased your purchasing power and possibly result in you purchasing more from them.

* Former employers, colleagues, or co-workers

Maintaining a good relationship with previous employers and colleagues has more benefits than you can imagine. This is the reason most people try their best to iron out any difficulties with their previous employers, even if they are no longer associated with the company.

Aside from the possibility that your potential employer will call previous employers when they review your job history, former employers and colleagues are also a good source of information related to that field.

When you ask for help from family and friends, there is the possibility that the information they can give you is just from another source. They may not be able to give you first-hand information or detailed information unless they also work in the same field that you came from or would like to go into.

This is different when you consult former employers and colleagues from the same sector. They will be able to provide you with valuable information and may be able to clarify information and answer your questions.

* Members of your professional organization

If you belong to a professional organization related to the field in which you are looking for a job, you can consult the organization for current posting from the members. If you don't belong to any, consider joining one since this will be beneficial to your career growth.

A professional organization can provide you with information from its members on current job openings. The organization can also give you details on the company profile and even on current market and career trends.

These are the most important people you should include when creating a list of your warm contacts. It is better if you contact as many as possible, so you can have as many options in your job search as possible. When you talk to them, tell them you are actively seeking a job.

Tips on Using Your Warm Contact List When Networking

These warm contacts can provide you with up-to-date information on the company and position vacancies that may not be posted on job ads. At times when they cannot provide you with information about a job you're looking for, they may be able to refer you to a person they know who may be able to tell you something about a job. This is called networking.

Networking is when you start using your warm list to get information or referrals from their contacts. Many people are repelled by the thought of networking. Some believe it is not a reliable source of information about a job. Others say networking is more difficult than following the leads on the ads posted in the newspaper, internet, or job boards.

Contrary to such beliefs, networking is not that difficult to do. You may just have to contact or meet some people, and you can get valuable information that can help in your career search. Also, since the people you meet belong to different industries, they can provide information about hiring that isn't advertised and first-hand facts about the company.

You may already be networking and you just don't know it. Have you seen an ad in the paper posted by a company you know little about and asked a friend if they know somebody who works for the company? So, even if you are not interested by the idea of networking, it is essential when seeking a job. To make networking easier and more productive for you, here are a few tips.

TIPS!

* Prepare your warm contact list.

When you have prepared your contact list, it will be easier to select the people who you prefer to call first. These are the people who you think have some information about a job. They may be former employers, colleagues, or members of the professional organization belonging to the same industry. They usually have first-hand, up-to-date, and reliable information.

* Calling a warm contact

When you call a warm contact, inform

them that you are actively seeking a job. Ask them to let you know if they hear of job openings you might be interested in. It is better to inform them of what type of job you are looking for.

Don't forget to leave your contact number with them, so they can get in touch with you if they hear of anything. It is also better if you can provide them with a copy of your résumé, so they can show or submit it to someone who will be able to help you in your job search.

* Assess yourself before calling your contact.

Your warm contact may ask about your skills, experiences, abilities, interests, expectations, and career goals. You should be able to talk about these sincerely, and you should be able to describe what information you would like to have from your contact.

To help you prepare, review your

Master Résumé. That way, you can articulate what you would like to communicate to your warm contact.

Anticipate questions about yourself, so you should also practice answering questions about your previous job and what you can contribute to the company.

* Ask for referrals.

If your warm contact was not able to provide information that will be helpful to your job search, ask for the names of at least two people who they think will be able to help you. Ask for their contact number and, if possible, the time they will be free to talk over the phone.

* Contact referrals immediately.

When your warm contact gives you referrals, they may even call this person to inform them that you will be asking for more information. Sometimes, the person you were referred to will call your warm contact. Therefore, it is better to call your referrals within a few days after you have spoken with your warm contact.

When you make a call, introduce yourself and inform the person who referred you to him/her and how you know the person who referred you. Be polite, but straightforward, when informing the person of what information you're seeking.

Networking really isn't a difficult thing to do. With enough practice and experience, you can maximize the benefits you can get from networking.

How to Get Referrals from Warm Contacts

You may find it hard to use networking to find a job if you can't rely on your warm contacts to give you the information you need. At times, you may have to ask your warm contacts to refer you to at least two people they know who will be able to give you the information you need.

However, there are times when your warm contact, particularly those who don't know you well, may not readily provide you with the information. Some of your warm contacts may feel reluctant to vouch for you to their other contacts; because of this, you may find it difficult to use your network. To make networking and getting referrals an easy task for you, here are a few tips.

TIPS!

* Nurture your warm contacts.

Before you even need your warm contacts or before you even ask for help, keep in touch with your warm contacts. You may send notes or greetings from time to time, call to "catch up", invite them to lunch, be interested or help in their business, or do anything just to cultivate your connection with them. By the time you need help, they can remember you and can more readily give information about their other contacts that will be able to help you.

I suggest you check in with people you have in your contacts every once in a while; birthdays and holidays are good times to call or simply send a text or message on social media. Building a friendship with others is valuable, not just reaching out when you need a favor.

Really work to build a meaningful relationship, so when you need a job, a reference letter, or a favor, you have a group of people that wouldn't mind helping, and of course, you have to be willing to offer the same to them.

Once you start to grow in your career and continue to meet new people you keep in touch with, you will start to find networking is much easier with a long list of warm contacts that you consider friends.

* Be polite.

Since you might not have close personal relationships with some of your valuable warm contacts, you may feel it's inappropriate to give them a call and ask them for information about your field of interest. Sometimes, sending a note in advance or asking to meet them for lunch is a better way to ask for their help.

* Listen to them.

Most of the time, even if your warm contact knows little in the field where you're trying to find a job, they might offer you advice. Be polite and interested in what they are saying. Who knows? The information they're giving may be valuable to you in the future.

There are times when your warm contacts may give you tips on what to do when you talk to the person to whom you're being referred. Your warm contacts may also imply what qualities and qualifications the person is looking for.

* Ask for at least two referrals.

Two referrals are enough from each warm contact. This is to have another option in case the first one didn't work. Asking for more than two referrals could be impolite as it can take more time from your warm contact. Also, that will make your warm contact feel you are relying mostly on him or her for your job search. So, unless they volunteer the information, don't ask for more than two referrals.

Before you ask for referrals, make sure your warm contact said everything that he or she can say about your field of interest. Even if they know little about that field, it is impolite if you cut them short while they're speaking to ask if they know someone who will be able to help you.

If they weren't able to refer you to at

least one of their contacts, thoughtfully ask them why they couldn't do so if you like. They may give you answers that may include indirect comments or suggestions. They may also indicate a lack of confidence in your work strategy. If this is so, you may have to make follow ups with them to prove you're credible.

However, there are also times when they can't refer you to their contacts, because they just don't know anybody who might have the information to help you.

In this case, ask them to keep their eyes open for opportunities that you might be interested in. You can also provide them with copies of your résumé. If you're given referrals, contact them as soon as possible.

Cold Calling

There's a little Girl Scout on the street carrying boxes of different flavored cookies, timidly trying to knock on her neighbors' doors, worried that doors will just slam shut in her face after offering her cookies for just a few dollars. Such a pitiful sight, right?

But imagine what this little girl could be feeling even before approaching doors. Will they know that she is on official business and is selling cookies for the good of humanity? Will she be able to say her rehearsed cookie selling script? Will she make her first sell?

Little does she know that a lot of grown-ups, even professional salesmen, experience the same anxiety, the idea of making their own cold call. It's normal to feel butterflies in your belly just thinking of making a call (whether personal or business).

But, let me give you the exact explanation of what a cold call is. A cold call is a personal call; it can be a visit or phone call to someone you know a little or someone you really don't know. The main reason for the call is that you are selling something for personal or official business.

Others think a cold call is only being made to total strangers, taken from phone lists or referrals from other people. On the contrary, this cold call can be made to someone you already know or to a prospect you're already familiar with. It can be someone you met last month at a party or maybe a friend introduced you and you found this person to be a good prospect for future use. But still, contacting someone you know breaks the ice for a moment.

Try to narrow your prospects at first until you feel comfortable. Once you've mastered the technique, it's time to move on to more challenging prospects you never even thought of approaching.

When you start to make your cold

calls, the whole ordeal may make you feel like quitting everything. Even professionals, like doctors, lawyers and professors, feel the same, which is why they depend on friends or clients' referrals for fear of losing their dignity and good name after making an unsuccessful cold call.

Nothing can be as uncomfortable as prospecting someone for your cold call. The fear of being shouted at or making a fool of yourself is a roadblock and keeps you from networking. This can be overcome with the right attitude, together with planning, preparation, and if possible - training. Believe it or not, salesmanship is possible for everyone. In this case, your product is yourself.

Take these simple tips on how to Cold Call

Always be Positive

Remember that cold calling is a powerful

networking strategy. First, be positive! There must be enthusiasm in your voice that people can feel right away.

I am what I am

Try not to sound obviously nervous whether on the phone or in person. Never try to be somebody you're really not with an aim to getting the attention you need. Assume that talking to your prospective contact for the first time should be the key to a lasting relationship.

Calm Down

Cold calls are difficult to make. Being well-prepared will help minimize the magnitude of the cold call. Take a deep breath and call.

Online. When it comes to job searching methods, the internet will be your most vital tool. Using the internet is the next best method to use after networking during your job search. The internet allows you to visit and apply to multiple job sites in a few short hours from the comfort of your home.

There are many job websites that post jobs, but keep in mind that, due to the ease of these sites, you will be up against local, national, or even international competition. Visit these sites on a regular basis, but use the other listed methods as well. Most companies do not have a person looking through all the initial resumes. Many companies use computer systems that sort through the applications before the hiring personnel do, so use the same verbiage as the job announcement to get past this system.

Many companies also do not utilize the job websites, so visit the company websites that interest you. Companies usually have a career or job opportunities page with the vacancies listed.

Newspapers. Many newspapers are now available online for free. Applying at

 several companies initially in a local area can save an applicant more time and money. If it so happens that a job was found late in the day, call immediately for inquiries and never let a day pass when opportunities arise. Local newspapers provide "help wanted" classifieds. Most newspapers are now free online, and this will help you scroll through many local classifieds without having to buy the daily issue.

Direct Employer Contact/Yellow pages. Sometimes, companies and employers do not advertise any job openings in their organization. The best thing for an applicant to do is submit an application or résumé. If the company isn't hiring at the

moment, ask that they keep it on file if possible.

Doing your job search directly could result in a lot of effort and no results. Look for "Now Hiring" signs, and whenever you're in a business, simply asking, "Are you hiring?" would be sufficient. Be observant of signs posted on doors, vehicles, and windows of shops around you. Just walk in and ask for information about the job and how to apply. Always have a résumé with you; you never know when an opportunity will present itself.

Even if you wouldn't work in that business, still ask. This is not only a way to network, but it gets you in the habit of asking. Looking through the yellow pages will open your mind to the local businesses and the career opportunities you may have never thought about.

Thinking like there's no box will help

you limit competition and increase the chances of an interview. Oftentimes, the Yellow Pages does the important job of providing information on how and where to call to look for a job. This gives an accurate list of companies and prospective employers in a chosen area. Contact these employers personally, even if they did not advertise any vacant positions that need to be filled. I feel that job searching is a numbers game, and the more you put out, the closer you will get to your goal.

Temporary Agencies. Temporary or "Temp" agencies are another great way to job search. Many temp agencies are now facing a higher volume of job seekers, so please shop around for the best fit. A word of advice would be not to use a particular temp agency if a fee is required on your part. Never pay for a job. Search for agencies that receive compensation from the employer.

Job Fairs. Job Fairs have changed over the past few years, and many simply refer you to apply online. Getting out and attending a job fair will help you network, build confidence, and practice effective communication skills. You can find upcoming job fairs using an internet search engine.

Unemployment/One-Stop Centers. These centers help with all your job search needs including but not limited to faxing your résumé and other documents to employers, job search workshops, and using the internet for employment purposes. These centers may also be the place where unemployment benefits are filed. Include this method in your job search, because they have many valuable resources for the active job seeker.

Library. Visiting the library is also a tool that can be useful when looking for a job. There are libraries that have a list of local employers, community resources, and more; just ask the librarian for more information.

How to be invited for Interviews

Apply Yourself

Résumé

Your résumé must present you very well. Seventy-five percent of employers say applicants with a résumé surpassing their standards would definitely be invited for a job interview. Some résumé tips that would open the door for more interviews include:

1. The position that an applicant is interested in should be placed right at the start of the résumé. Having this as an objective shows that an applicant is focused, career-oriented.

2. One of the most significant ways to get the employer's attention is by using

words that are powerful that denote strong capabilities of the applicant. An example of this is, instead of writing, "assigned to be", write "in-charge of," indicating the applicant has active leadership skills that can be a step to the management position if there is any.

3. A bullet catches the eye of an employer at one look. Use these when itemizing achievements, career highlights, recognitions, qualifications, skills, and interests. Words in bullet form guide the employer to read the information provided. These also create more clear space on the paper, making the application or the résumé very neat and easy to read.

4. Make sure the résumé is selective. Only apply for a certain position in one company or organization one at a time. Do not submit résumés with different job interests and positions at one time.

5. Use résumé paper; it's thicker than

the standard printer paper and will help your résumé stand out if submitting a paper résumé. Keep to just one to two pages in length, because you have a lot of competition, and employers don't have a lot of time. Look at adjusting your margin settings when typing your résumé to have more space.

6. Have someone else proofread your résumé. Correct spelling and grammar are critical.

Completing applications and cover letters.

Many people put a great amount of effort into their resumes; some even pay top dollar for what they feel best shows off what they can do. After spending so much time on your resume, many fail to put the same time and dedication into completing their application and cover letters. Applications and cover letters are an important piece of your job search; please don't underestimate the power these two pieces have when obtaining a job.

Applications:

Think about an application from the employer's side. It's a document that's standard and has all the desired information for everyone. Isn't that easier than looking at all different types of resumes in different formats? I would like to think so. An application asks for all the things an employer needs, which is also on your resume, right? The difference is it's standardized.

The employer asks for your name, address, phone, job history, and education on your application without looking at your resume, and they can ask specific questions related to that particular job and company. It's important to apply what you learned in this handbook to the application process as well.

Everything you do with the customized resume, simply use the same information when you fill out the application. Use the same accomplishments listed for each job in the job history section of your application and remember to use the same job announcement verbiage.

Cover Letters:

A Cover Letter is the one true place to show who you are and what you can bring. This is a great place to apply the thinking like there's no box approach (discussed in a later section). Try to stay away from the standard cover letter examples, because this is where you must stand out to be remembered to get the interview.

You have to make the employer want to interview you. Some things that I have used in the past are having a bullet section highlighting my qualifications needed for the job I'm applying for. This will help the employer see you have what they want. Ensure your letter doesn't contain any grammar or spelling errors and it's interesting to read.

Customize the letter to the job by listing the hiring manager name if known, company name, and the position you're applying to. Another suggestion is, at the bottom of the letter, write a P.S. note. Have you ever seen a P.S. note at the bottom of a cover letter? Most employers probably haven't, and that makes you different.

Online Applications:

Aside from preparing an impressive résumé, carefully follow and read all the special instructions, like how many spaces are provided for a specific answer or the number of words for the answer. Keep in mind that this is also a test to see how well an applicant can follow simple rules. Not only do you have to follow the steps, but the application should also be neat. If this is a paper application, handwriting is also being considered, and using a black pen will greatly add to the formality of the answer. As much as possible, never use white out or bend the application. If possible, complete your application online.

When answering, be careful not to leave blanks unless it does not apply. Use N/A only if necessary. Be truthful with all answers, but this does not mean you have to provide a complete or thorough answer for every question. Always adapt the answers to the job being applied for. Only provide the skills and recognition received that will be beneficial to the new company or employer. However, see to it that the answers provided indicate the reason you are more qualified than the other applicants.

Choose references that can provide value to your success in obtaining the job. Possible references could be teachers, friends, and previous employers. The application must be consistent with the résumé. Since many of these employers standardize and gauge the information the applicant is providing in his/her application and résumé, these must be full of complete and honest information.

The application will ask personal questions, but always be truthful. If you have some negative responses on your application, remember you still have the opportunity to get an interview and maybe even the job offer. For example, if you have been convicted of a felony or misdemeanor, just be honest and, if given the chance to interview, know how to sell the benefits that the employer will receive from hiring you.

Many states offer a tax break to

employers that hire those with a criminal record. Know the programs available and be prepared to explain them to the employer. Many employers are unaware of how it works and the benefits until you educate them. An example of these programs is the Federal Bonding Program. I recommend doing a google search on 'Federal Bonding Program' for more details and don't stop there. Look for other programs as well.

❖ TASK: Track your progress (template provided)

After submitting applications and résumés to the respective companies, keep track of the progress by creating a chart where you can jot down the name of the company and when the application was submitted, job applied for, and login information if online.

TIP: *Apply the following tips when completing online applications*

When applying online, use the following tips:

Complete your sentences and do not abbreviate

Employers do not like when you submit applications and cover letters that seem casual. It is important to remain professional throughout the job seeking process. Your written interactions should always be formal and well-written. This gives a good impression regarding your capabilities and skills.

Get directly to the point

When completing an application or writing a cover letter, you must be concise and straightforward. Do not put a story in the letter just to get the attention of the employer. Chances are he or she will just get irritated with you, and this only reduces your chances of getting hired.

Instead, state the most valuable and relevant information. In today's job market, competition is overwhelming, which make employers overwhelmed with applicants, so just state the facts.

Consider potential issues that may hinder you from getting the job

You may find instances when you lack the experiences the position requires. Review the job announcement and review your Master Résumé to decide if you have the skills and experience the job announcement states. Some jobs may require a lot of experience; some may have no barriers to entry but the job may entail a routine work flow.

As long as you have the education requirements, it's important that you present yourself in a way that proves you're capable of fulfilling the job duties.

Getting the job you want may be a challenge but never lose hope

It is better to wait a while and get a job that you will enjoy, rather than get a job as soon as possible but ending up dissatisfied and unhappy. State your goals on paper and go for it. Job searching during this current time has made job seekers feel defeated. Stay motivated and positive and your goals will soon manifest.

TIP: Use Résumé Paper for your resumes (the thickness with help to make your résumé stand out)

Checking for mistakes. With the current trend of technology and its merging with business processes, more companies are now requiring prospective applicants to submit their application online to include a cover letter, résumé, and references.

Thus, first impressions are relayed not only by your first appearance, but also the quality and content of your online communications. E-mails, applications, cover letters, and all written material regarding a job should be polished and well-articulated. Use the dictionary, a spelling checker, and have a friend proofread your work before you submit your items to the employer.

Check your résumé for mistakes. Before submitting your résumé to a prospective employer, check it for errors at least three times before handing it over. Spelling and grammatical errors are serious no-no's. After researching the job position, it is critical that you format your résumé to match the needs of the company. For example, if you are applying for an accounting job, you should put your accounting experience in detail on your résumé.

It is also ideal to keep the length of the résumé to a page or two. If you need an additional page, please use at least half of the second page and include your name and number if the pages are separated on top of the additional pages. It is important to match your résumé language with the verbiage used in the job announcement when submitting your résumé online.

Many companies use a computer system to separate the candidates by narrowing down the list for the hiring personnel. The system's job is basically to find the closest match to the job announcement and allow those applicants to pass on to the next level. Using this technique will increase the chances that the hiring personnel will review your application.

Once an application is sent and the résumé has been received, the next thing that would possibly happen is that the employer will call to test communication skills by means of an interview. If you're contacted by an employer, this only means they were impressed with the documents submitted; therefore, they are interested in a personal interview with you.

Part Two: GET THE JOB!

Interviewing Skills

In the midst of technological advancement nowadays, the "back-to-basics" rule still applies when it comes to getting hired for a job. It does not matter if you are planning to apply to a million-dollar company or a small, independent firm. When you face an interviewer, it all boils down to how you present yourself. This is the deciding factor whether you will get hired.

So, you have distributed your résumé to prospective employers and you have determined the correct jobs to apply for. The next step is to be prepared for the possible interviews.

You may make the acquaintance of the assistant or the receptionist when being scheduled for an interview, either by phone or email. Be friendly and polite, as these people might provide information that can be essential to getting that job or give you a background of the company or your prospective boss.

Finally, you show up for the interview.

The basic traits of being prompt, how

you speak and carry yourself, and how you dress are all factors that contribute to making a lasting impression that will eventually get you hired.

Here are 7 easy steps to improve your interviewing skills:

1.) Prepare for the interview.

Research the company, review your answers to possible interview questions, decide what to wear, review the time, and location.

Before the interview. Once you've received a call for an interview, now is the time to prepare for the interview. Write down the time and date of the scheduled interview. While on the phone with the employer, try to get as much information as possible about the interview.

Some helpful information to make note of would be the company, position, the exact location (building, address, room number), what to bring, dress code, contact person, and parking details. It's helpful to ask that an email is sent with the interview details if possible.

Once you have this information, review details about the company and the position you applied for. I would also suggest reviewing your Master Résumé, because you never know what questions you will be asked during the interview. You can usually find details about most companies on the internet. Review their website and be sure to take a look at the mission & vision statements. Do a mock interview with a friend or family member if you feel it will prepare you for the upcoming interview.

A survey conducted by a staffing and consulting firm based in California that corresponded with 1,400 chief financial officers concluded that candidates for employment made most of their mistakes on their interviews. Some mistakes they made include:

- Arriving late
- Having little knowledge about the company
- Having little knowledge about the position applied for
- Having a superiority complex
- Behaving arrogantly

What should you take from this? Be on time, know about the company and the position, look nice, try to be relax, and be yourself.

Dress appropriately. Once the interviewer walks into the room, or once you walk into the room to be interviewed, your appearance will be the first thing to make an impact. Dress appropriately, check your grooming, and mind your posture. Read the section on dressing for success!

Second, practice basic courtesy. Know where the interview will be held and be there with ample time to prepare yourself before the scheduled interview. Turn your phone off to avoid unnecessary distractions.

Dressing for the interview

First impressions last, so the way an applicant looks really does matter. Employers could easily decide based on the manner in which you dress during the initial interview.

Better questions and service can be received if your appearance commands respect. It is important to consider the surrounding of the company granting you an interview. There is no reason to be overdressed or poorly dressed during this significant day.

In fact, it is a good rule of thumb to dress appropriately for any situation. Some might say the inner characteristics of the person matter more, but in reality, you only have one opportunity for a first impression. Make it count!

TIP: *Top things to DO when getting ready for your interview*

DO have clean and neat fingernails.

DO wear jewelry that doesn't rattle and jiggle as you speak and move. Try not to wear two or more rings or earrings. If you have piercings aside from the ears, be mindful about the job you're applying for and what your appearance is saying.

DO have a professional and well-groomed hairdo/haircut.

DO wear closed shoes.

DO remember that a good suit or dress brings more confidence as well.

DO avoid short skirts.

DO wear appropriate blazers.

DO wear a tie. If there is no suit and tie available, use a collared shirt or white long sleeves.

DO be cautious of how much perfume, cologne, or aftershave you're using.

DO use a briefcase or padfolio in perfect condition to bring your two-three interview questions, personal information, and résumé.

The way a person looks should equal the message he or she is trying to convey. During the interview, this can become either a plus factor for the applicant or a big loss. Know that an applicant should look appealing, fashionable but not loud.

Consider the latest trends in the area or location where the prospective job is located. One aspect in which the employer picks a new hire is based on the physical attributes of the applicant. You're being rated from the moment the employer sees you, and things like how you shook hands, keep attentive eye contact, your posture, your smile, and even how you dressed are all being rated.

Regardless of your personal career background, skills, and underlying talents, if the first impression was not striking enough to make an outstanding impression on the interviewers, nothing else counts. This can be the potential employers' initial interpretation of how an applicant will do on the job. Whether that perception is "fair" is irrelevant. Do you want the job? Look the part and your chances for success are much greater!

2.) Research.

Use all your resources to make sure

you know the basics about the company. You would not want to be caught unprepared when asked about how you heard or what you know about the company you're applying for.

Learn about your potential employer. In your mind, develop a clear picture of the company profile.

Make sure you prepared answers to a few basic questions but do not sound scripted. This happens when you rehearse what you will be saying word for word. It is enough that you have an overview of what you will share with the interviewer, and it is better to be spontaneous.

During the interview. The body language of the applicant must also denote that he/she is confident yet not overpowering. Remember to maintain eye contact, have a firm handshake, and avoid looking defensive by crossing your arms.

Wearing the right clothes is crucial for projecting a confident stance. As they say, it is better to go to an interview over-dressed than be under-dressed.

3.) Be cool.

Make a great first impression by maintaining eye contact, giving the interviewer a firm handshake, a friendly smile, and a polite greeting. Sit only when you are asked to do so and do not forget to thank the interviewer for taking time out of his or her busy schedule to interview you. Make sure to start on a positive note and set the proper expectations.

4.) Do not sell yourself short.

In the course of the interview, answer the questions briefly and accurately. The key is to be honest.

Make sure that, as a prospective employee, you share with your future employer who you really are and what you can do for the company. Stay positive and do not give a bad impression about your previous employers.

If you are applying for your first job, do not let your lack of experience hinder you from gaining the advantage against more experienced applicants. What you lack in experience, make up for in confidence and eagerness to learn.

You may also put yourself in the employer's shoes. Ask yourself, if I were on the other side of this desk, what qualities should I look for in a potential employee? Would I profit if he works for me, and can he contribute to the development of the company?

Do not be afraid to sell yourself but do not be overconfident. Just project a picture that you are sure of yourself and your capabilities.

5.) Ask questions.

Have a question or two to ask the interviewer. This lets the employer know you are also looking for the right fit.

Answer questions smartly

A common mistake of interviewees is that they tend to get tense and forget the questions that are given to them, which gives the impression that they are not prepared for the interview. For this reason, it is important to review your Master Résumé, research the company and the position to prevent being side-tracked during the interview.

If you do not know the answer to the questions being asked, it is better to admit you don't know the answer to the question and add that you can do some research about it.

When researching the company, look for the skills or expertise the company is looking for so that, when the interview day comes and the interviewer asks about your strengths and core competencies, you will be able to express your skills that match what they need. Also have one or two questions to ask the interviewer if they ask if you have any questions.

6.) Wrap it up.

As you near the end of the interview, make sure all bases are covered. During the interview isn't the time to discuss or even ask about the salary and the benefits you will receive once employed. The time for that will be once you're offered the position and discussing the job offer.

If the employer brings it up first, then it's appropriate for you to ask questions and express your needs. If you must know the salary and can't wait until the job is offered, ask the employer about the benefits, which usually opens the door for the employer to share the salary. Try not to push the issue, though.

Wrap things up by summarizing your strengths and pointing out your positive traits. Ask about the next steps in the hiring process. Finally, as you end the interview, make sure to thank the interviewer again for his or her time, leaving a lasting impression.

❖ *TASK:* *Get the interviewer's business card; this will allow you to spell the person's name correctly and have their contact information for the follow up thank you note or card.*

7.) Follow up.

Send that all-important thank you note or card after the interview. Thank the interviewer for the time that he or she took with you and for giving you the opportunity to interview. Make sure you know who to contact for follow-up of the results. Send the thank you note or card right after the interview.

TIPS: *If you are still looking for a job, here are some tips on how to follow up on your contacts:*

* Send a thank you note or card right after the interview. This is a way of getting the prospective employer to hear from you again. Should you not get hired for the current position they are offering, someone from that company will likely keep your information on file for future consideration.
* Make sure you leave your phone number and email address, so prospective employers will have no excuse of not getting in touch with you.
* Be accurate in getting the contact information of perspective employers to ensure their information is correct when you send them your thank you note.
* Some companies take a look at your

character references, so alert the people on your list that they might receive a call from your prospective employers.

* Always be on the positive side. Should you not get hired for a particular position, you may ask the people from that company for any improvements that you could make or at least keep you in mind for future hiring.

How to Follow Up on All Contacts

An important part of the job search process is to follow up on all contacts/people you meet while networking. It is not good just to sit and wait for results to come pouring in when you think you've already done your part because your contact information has been distributed.

Consider two men applying for a prime position at a company. After the interview, the first applicant just sits around waiting to hear from his prospective employer.

On the other hand, the second applicant distributes his contact information to some people that he met in the company. Furthermore, applicant number two does a follow-up call a few days later. The first applicant has not been heard from, because he just doesn't follow up. Who do you think will have a greater chance of getting the job?

Let's say the first applicant is more qualified, but if he did not follow up, in the end, he may not get the job offer.

If you are still waiting for that job offer and you do not follow up on your contacts, your chances of getting hired become slimmer. In business, following up on all your contacts is a sure-fire way to spread the word about you, your business sense, and your expanding horizons.

Jobseeker FAQs on Thank You notes

Career advisers tell jobseekers to send a thank you note or card after an interview. In regard to the most frequently asked questions on how and what to send in a thank you note, here are some answers.

Won't the employer think that an applicant is desperate if he sends a thank you letter?

Of course not. Rarely is an employer not pleased to receive a thank you letter. It is considered a common way of showing politeness, a gesture of courtesy, one way to outshine the rest of the interviewees, and a way to keep your name upfront.

Will it jeopardize the possibility of getting the job?

Most employers waver between the last two most promising applicants. If you lack experience, then you need to make all the difference you can. A simple gesture, like a thank you note, can land you the job.

However, applicants who were almost on the verge of being hired but suddenly hit the skids after sending in a bad thank you note can do more harm than good. A bad thank you note can jeopardize your possibilities of getting the job. Be aware of grammar errors, because the thank you note is not only a great way to set yourself apart but it also shows you have good communication skills. Being able to write effectively is definitely a desired trait for many companies.

Can it be handwritten or should it be typed?

Actually, it does not matter. What's important is doing it. It must be tailored to your prospective company and the person who interviewed you. Thus, respect is further established. However, if the company, interviewer, or the position demands a formal business letter, then do so. Mostly, a handwritten note is okay if the interviewer and the applicant have built rapport.

Will it be okay to e-mail the thank you note?

Yes, email is fine. If the people in the company use e-mail in all their communication and correspondence, then it should be acceptable. This will also apply if the company is into fast decision making when hiring applicants. Always remember that, even if emails fit in with the culture of the company, it's still a better idea to follow up the email with a hard copy of your thank you.

Will a borrowed thank you letter do?

Yes, borrowing is one thing. But make sure to look at the basic structure of the letter. Never plagiarize the whole letter as it may be applicable to one person but not for the other. Surely, there are employers who can distinguish a thank you note that has been copied. Look online for sample letters, but make it your own.

If it was a panel interview, should thank you letters be sent to all interviewers?

Frankly, that's the best. The same letter to each is as essential as making one for each. All you have to do is edit some phrases for individuality.

How soon should a thank you note be sent?

The golden rule is to send thank you notes within 24 hours after the interview.

Will it still be okay to mail the thank you note if the hiring decision will be made sooner than when the mailed thank you note is received?

If you think the mail will be received

after the hiring decision has been made, then find a faster way: it can be via email, fax, express delivery, or personal delivery. If you have to hand deliver the thank you note, it can leave a great impression.

Thinking Like There's No Box

How can one person "think like there's no box"? This should be done independently, but how? Here's an example: Cut a cake into eight slices, but you have to make no more than three cuts. Most people will have trouble coming up with a way to cut the cake. But to solve this, you have to change the way you look at the cake and how to cut it. One perfect solution is to cut the cake into two equal sizes and put the other half on top of the other. Cut it again in half then stack the other half pieces on top of one another and cut them again. There you go; that's thinking like there's no box.

Think of ways that the lazy job seeker wouldn't do and do them. Maybe consider having a website about you and your skills for the employer to visit and see how innovative you are. This would work great if you have to display a portfolio to employers or things that you created to display them in action. Think of ways to disrupt the job market and be noticed.

The job search process takes determination and patience. With the current unemployment rates, competition for job openings has increased tremendously. You have to stay organized and consistent. Be prepared to receive many disappointing letters, but if you fully apply yourself, you will land the employment that meets your needs.

Review this handbook, complete the tasks, and make note of the tips. As you gain new skills and experience and progress through life, remember to help those that follow by sharing information.

REMEMBER

- You will become discouraged, but continue to motivate yourself. Have a support team behind you that believes in you, even when you don't. Stay focused; don't give up.
- Know yourself. Understand your needs and wants and don't settle for less.
- Sell yourself- wear your best. Your best doesn't have to be fancy, expensive clothing. Shop smart and on a budget. Department stores have great items on clearance and don't forget about the nice things you see in thrift stores and dollar stores. Be clean, wear little to no cologne/fragrance, and groom

yourself as though it's your wedding day.

- Make a great first impression both over the phone and in person.
- Give a firm handshake, never assume anything, give good eye contact, and be confident.
- Be the nice version of you.
- Silence your cell phone prior to interviews.
- Be on time….which is 20 minutes before the scheduled time, to find the correct area, parking, and to calm yourself.
- Always be professional……ensure this is the case when it comes to your personal voicemails, emails, Facebook/Instagram(social media), and phone etiquette in general.
- The internet is the best sources

for...........any and everything.

- Networking, using the yellowpages, newspapers, internet (company website), direct contact-walk-ins, local career center, and staffing agencies, are places to look for jobs.
- Always have some résumés on résumé paper with you.
- Customize your résumés using the same verbiage in the job announcement, especially if online.
- Use apps, technology, Google autofill extensions, and automation tools to make the job process faster and easier.
- Keep a record of all the jobs you applied for and keep track of the usernames/passwords for each job website.
- Stand out from the crowd by thinking like there's no box. Have a great

résumé (one to two pages,
professional, and no spelling/grammar
errors), résumé paper, send thank you
notes, and present yourself well.

- Be honest but don't supply more than
  what's asked.

Now go get started!!! Get the Interview! Get the Job! You now know where to start. Stay focused and remain motivated. With determination and persistence, you will get the interview and job you want.

Thank you for purchasing this book. Please visit theHiredProject.com for more information, free resources, tips, and posted blog posts.

Examples and Templates

Job Tracker Worksheet

Company	Location	Phone Number	Position	Date Applied	Online Username and Password	Website

Sample Résumé

JANE DOE
12123 Pine Street
Washington, DC 20012
(202) 555-5532
janedoe20012@gmail.com

Highlights of Qualifications

- Over 15 years of experience providing administrative, management, and program support skills in the health care field
- Developed policies and procedures for the efficient operation of two programs
- Developed training materials and presented information within an organization of over 7,000 employees

WORK EXPERIENCES:

Healthcare Administrator   **July 2000- Present**
George Washington University Hospital, Washington, DC
- Ensures compliance with Department of Health and other regulatory standards and maintains all related documentation
- Manages financial resources effectively and maintains compliance with budgetary goals and constraints
- Participates in Quality Assurance and Improvement activities, in collaboration with the Medical Director
- Assures consistency in the identification, reporting, analysis, and prevention of adverse incidents.
- Follows the commitment to excellence and treats patients, families, visitors and each other with courtesy, dignity, respect and professionalism.
- Oversees all personnel activities, including recruitment, training, high-level supervision and retention of employees.
- Prepare, submit, and manage grant proposals to obtain funding for needed program items and supplies.

Administrative Assistant   **January 1995- July 2000**
John Hopkins Medical Center
- Proactively supported 12 assigned leaders and their teams by independently handling all assigned duties, taking direction from and balancing the needs of multiple staff members.
- Handled confidential data and matters in a discreet and professional manner.
- Maintained and coordinated calendars, schedule appointments and meetings (including both onsite and off-site conference arrangements), arrange travel schedules, travel itineraries, reconcile T&L expenses for 12 leaders.
- Maintained over 2000 risk files, keeping organized and current; manage retrieval of files and maintain online systems and databases as required.

- Developed PowerPoint presentations, type letters, memos, charts, reports, proposals, agreements, or other types of correspondence and maintain records of all documents.
- Scheduled, planned, and organized all logistical details for in-house and off-site meetings, etc., as needed.
- Managed a wide range of general administrative services including: telephone coverage, documentation management/file set up and maintenance, photocopying, ordering office supplies, invoice processing.

EDUCATION:

Bachelor's Degree in Healthcare Administration

Georgetown University, GPA- 3.8

VOLUNTEER/SERVICES:

American Red Cross
Answer phones/administrative tasks

Sample Cover Letter

1/13/2019

Dear Interviewing Manager,

Thank you for taking the time to review my information. I'm interested in your organization and would like to be considered for the Senior Healthcare Administrator position. I'm seeking a career that will help build personal strength while working to be an asset to your organization. I feel your organization is a purposeful organization, and I would like to take my career to another level. I would like to be considered as part of your organization, because I feel I've found my purpose. I have over 15 years of experience in management, administration, healthcare, training and education and customer service while in private organizations. Additionally, I have special skills in budgeting, policies and procedure development, planning, and logistics.

HIGHLIGHTS OF QUALIFICATIONS:
- Over 15 years of experience providing administrative, management, and program support skills in the health care field

- Developed policies and procedures for the efficient operation of two programs

- Developed training materials and presented information within an organization of over 7,000 employees

- Performed program financial management services for two programs, including financial analysis, budget and cost quote preparation, cost management, reconciliation, and profit enhancement

- Over 10 years' experience developing and maintaining business relationships and coordinating outreach efforts

EDUCATION:

Bachelor's Degree in Healthcare Administration, Georgetown University, GPA- 3.8

Thank you again for your time.

Sincerely,

Jane Doe.
          Jane Doe

P.S. Thank you for taking the time to review my cover letter. I sincerely believe I'm a perfect fit for this position and your company. I look forward to speaking with you and thanks again for your consideration.

Sample Thank you Note

Dear Mr. Washington:

I sincerely enjoyed meeting with you yesterday and learning more about the Office Manager position at Daily's Department Store.

Our conversation confirmed my interest in becoming part of the Daily's Department Store staff. I was particularly pleased at the prospect of being able to develop my own profit improvement ideas with the regional manager and develop my business management skills.

I feel confident that my experiences in the workplace and in the classroom will enable me to fill the job requirements effectively.

Please feel free to contact me if I can provide you with any further information. I look forward eagerly to hearing from you, and thank you again for the courtesy you extended to me.

Sincerely,

Jane Doe

Jane Doe

Since you read to the end, I would like to offer you some bonus advice:

Entrepreneurship

Now that you have finished this handbook on getting the interview, getting the job, I challenge you to ask yourself if working for someone else is truly what you would like to do. The job market is very competitive and even harder as you get older, gain more experience, or if you have a criminal background. In today's world, millionaires are being made every day from online businesses. You can literally start a business with little to no capital.

I encourage you to explore the possibilities of being an entrepreneur. Everyone has a talent, invention, or idea that is worth money to others, and with the internet at your fingertips, you could invest in your own dreams and make yourself wealthy, instead of making others wealthy, trading your time for cash. Doing the latter will result in you finding yourself at retirement age with very little retirement money.

A lifetime of labor and you have to live a life you did not dream of, but those people you work for years with your time and body has endless amounts of money. I want to be clear; entrepreneurship isn't for everyone, and yes, we do need people to be the worker bees, but if you are finding it hard to get a decent job, because of that criminal record that you already did time for at a different time in your life, then you may have to create your own means to survive when others don't want to give you a decent opportunity.

I say use your time to apply to jobs and figure out how you could build something that will produce more for you and your family for the future. When it comes to a job search, a bad yearly review, a smudge on your record, sexism, ageism, many applicants, and many other factors outside of you being able to do the job could be a hindrance to you even getting an interview. Just food for thought.